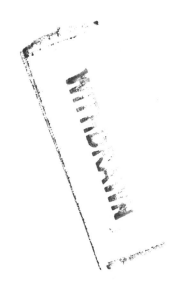

I R I S H
IN AMERICA

web enhanced at www.inamericabooks.com

MARGARET J. GOLDSTEIN

⌐ LERNER PUBLICATIONS COMPANY / MINNEAPOLIS

Current information and statistics quickly become out of date. That's why we developed **www.inamericabooks.com**, a companion website to the **In America** series. The site offers lots of additional information—downloadable photos and maps and up-to-date facts through links to additional websites. Each link has been carefully selected by researchers at Lerner Publishing Group and is regularly reviewed and updated. However, Lerner Publishing Group is not responsible for the accuracy or suitability of material on websites that are not maintained directly by us. It is recommended that students using the Internet be supervised by a parent, a librarian, a teacher, or other adult.

For Tom Collins Jr.—and the Irish of Chicago

Thanks to Tom Collins Sr., Phyllis Gaffney Fifield, and Marcie Walsh for providing insights into the lives of twentieth-century Irish immigrants.

Lerner Publications Company
A division of Lerner Publishing Group
241 First Avenue North
Minneapolis, MN 55401 U.S.A.

Website address: www.lernerbooks.com

Library of Congress Cataloging-in-Publication Data

Goldstein, Margaret J.
    Irish in America / by Margaret J. Goldstein.
        p.   cm. — (In America)
    Summary: Examines the history of Irish immigration to the United States, discussing why the Irish came, what their lives were like after they arrived, where they settled, and customs they brought from home.
    Includes bibliographical references and index.
    ISBN: 0-8225-3950-0 (lib. bdg. : alk. paper)
    1. Irish Americans—History—Juvenile literature. 2. Immigrants—United States—History—Juvenile literature. [1. Irish Americans—History.] I. Title. II. In America (Minneapolis, Minn.)
E184.I6 G65 2005
973'.049162—dc21   2002152930

Manufactured in the United States of America
1 2 3 4 5 6 – JR – 10 09 08 07 06 05

CONTENTS

INTRODUCTION

In America, a walk down a city street can seem like a walk through many lands. Grocery stores sell international foods. Shops offer products from around the world. People strolling past may speak foreign languages. This unique blend of cultures is the result of America's history as a nation of immigrants.

Native peoples have lived in North America for centuries. The next settlers were the Vikings. In about a.d. 1000, they sailed from Scandinavia to lands that would become Canada, Greenland, and Iceland. In 1492 the Italian navigator Christopher Columbus landed in the Americas, and more European explorers arrived during the 1500s. In the 1600s, British settlers formed colonies that, after the Revolutionary War (1775–1783), would become the United States. And in the mid-1800s, a great wave of immigration brought millions of new arrivals to the young country.

Immigrants have many different reasons for leaving home. They may leave to escape poverty, war, or harsh governments. They may want better living conditions for themselves and their children. Throughout its history, America has been known as a nation that offers many opportunities. For this reason, many immigrants come to America.

Moving to a new country is not easy. It can mean making a long, difficult journey. It means leaving home and starting over in an unfamiliar place. But it also means using skill, talent, and determination to build a new life. The In America series tells the story of immigration to the United States and the search for fresh beginnings in a new country—in America..

THE IRISH IN AMERICA

The flow of Irish immigrants to America began before the Revolutionary War—before the United States was even a nation. The numbers of immigrants from Ireland increased in the early 1800s but were still fairly low. Then in 1845, blight, or disease, destroyed Ireland's potato crop. Potatoes were the staple food of the Irish people. The blight caused a terrible famine—hundreds of thousands of people died of starvation and disease. With no hope for relief at home, desperate Irish peasants fled for their lives—most seeking refuge in the United States. More than one million Irish immigrants flooded onto American shores during the late 1840s and early 1850s.

The Irish came ashore in North America's port cities—most landing in New York City and Boston, Massachusetts. Bound together by their religion, Roman Catholicism, the Irish united through churches, schools, labor unions, and clubs. They eventually worked their way into the fabric of American society. The children and grandchildren of Irish immigrants gradually blended into the American mainstream. They climbed to the top levels of the nation's government, business, sports, and entertainment.

According to the U.S. Census, more than 33 million American citizens claim some Irish ancestry. Most of these Irish Americans have never lived in or even visited Ireland. In many cases, their families have lived in the United States for more than 150 years. These Americans still cherish their Irish roots and are proud of their heritage and culture.

1

THE EMERALD ISLE

Ireland, a small island west of England, is covered with rolling hills, rocky fields, and sparkling lakes. Lush and green, it is nicknamed the Emerald Isle. Its symbols include the shamrock, a kind of clover; the leprechaun, a mischievous little elf; and the Irish harp.

ANCIENT ROOTS

Ireland was first settled in about 6000 B.C., when people arrived there from the European mainland. About 400 B.C., a European group called the Celts conquered Ireland. They divided the island into many small kingdoms, which frequently warred with one another. Primarily farmers and shepherds, the Irish Celts spoke a language called Gaelic. They worshipped many gods. Their priests were called druids.

In A.D. 432, a religious teacher named Patrick arrived in Ireland. He was an English Christian who had previously lived in Ireland as a slave. After his escape from slavery,

Patrick set out to teach the Irish people about Christianity. First, he studied religion in France. He became a bishop and then returned to Ireland, where he founded more than three hundred churches. Patrick successfully brought the Irish people into his faith. He became the patron (guardian) saint of Ireland. His day of honor is March 17—Saint Patrick's Day.

Saint Patrick returned to Ireland, where he had escaped slavery, as a Christian missionary. In modern times, about 95 percent of Irish people are Roman Catholic.

INVASION AND PERSECUTION

Starting in the 800s, Vikings began to raid Ireland. The Vikings were fierce Scandinavian pirates, searching for land and riches. They attacked Irish villages and destroyed churches. Some Vikings settled permanently in Ireland, establishing towns along the seacoast. Finally, in 1014, an Irish king named Brian Boru fought back against the Vikings. He defeated them at the Battle of Clontarf. But even after this defeat, many Vikings remained in Ireland. They were gradually absorbed into the Irish population.

The next invaders came to Ireland from England, a powerful nation on an island east of Ireland. The English king, Henry II, sent soldiers into Ireland starting in the 1160s. Over the next one hundred years, English noblemen conquered most of Ireland. They brought elements of English culture to Ireland, including English laws and the English language. As English became more widespread in Ireland, Gaelic—the old language of the Celts—began to decline.

England's King Henry VIII, who ruled from 1509 to 1547, wanted to strengthen English control in Ireland. He declared himself king of Ireland in 1541. He sent soldiers and governors

English king Henry VIII took control of Ireland in 1541.

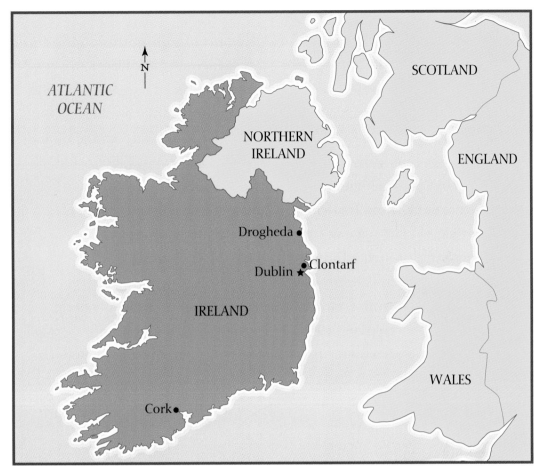

This map shows Ireland in relation to the modern-day countries of the United Kingdom: England, Wales, Scotland, and Northern Ireland. To downlad this and other maps, visit www.inamericabooks.com.

into Ireland and tried to make the Irish follow English laws. Henry also wanted the Irish to switch to the Protestant Church—the official church of England. The Irish people belonged to the Roman Catholic Church. The Protestant Church and the Roman Catholic Church were both Christian churches. But the two churches had different practices and beliefs.

The Irish people did not want to join the English church, and they did not want to be ruled by England. But Ireland was not a rich or powerful nation like England was. Most of its people were poor, uneducated farmers. They disliked the English, but they were unable to resist the powerful English government.

Queen Elizabeth I, Henry's daughter, continued her father's policies in Ireland. Elizabeth and her court viewed Catholicism, led by the pope in Rome, as a threat to England. To subdue this threat, she outlawed Catholic services in Ireland and executed some Catholic leaders. She also seized large amounts of Irish land and gave it to English Protestants. Elizabeth's successor, James I, seized more Irish land, mostly in the northern part of Ireland. He gave this land to both English and Scottish Protestants. As their lands were taken away, the Irish people fell further into poverty. Their mistrust of the English grew stronger.

In the late 1500s, the Irish began to revolt against English rule. A major rebellion raged from 1641 to 1649. Finally, English statesman

English cavalrymen (soldiers on horseback) attacked rebellious Irish using lances and other weapons during a revolt in Ireland in 1581.

*Oliver Cromwell led the English in defeating an
Irish rebellion in the mid-1600s.*

Oliver Cromwell crushed the Irish with a massacre at
Drogheda in the east of Ireland. Afterward, the
English cracked down even harder in Ireland. They
seized more land from Irish Catholics and stripped
Catholics of their rights. Under rules known as the
Penal Laws, Catholics were not allowed to own land,
vote, hold political office, serve in the military, teach
or attend school, speak Gaelic, or practice their
religion. The English shut down Catholic churches, but
Irish Catholics continued to worship in secret.

In the 1700s, Irish Catholics fought to regain
their rights. They had some success, and some of the
Penal Laws were abolished. But Ireland remained

A family is evicted from their home in Ireland.

under English control. By then Protestant noblemen, both English and Irish, owned most of the nation's farmland. They rented out tiny plots of ground to Irish peasants, who tried to eke out a living from the land. Rents were outrageously high—sometimes twice as high as those in England. Farmers paid their rent in crops instead of money. Those who couldn't pay were evicted—forced to leave their homes. Some of them starved to death.

EARLY AMERICANS

Conditions were harsh all over Ireland. At different times and in different places, people faced crop failure, drought, high rents, and unemployment. But there was talk that across the Atlantic Ocean, in the colonies of North America, people could make a fresh start. Starting in the early 1700s, people from the north of Ireland did just that. These people were members of an ethnic group called the Scotch-Irish. The Scotch-Irish were Protestants.

THE FIRST
IRISH AMERICAN?

Who was the first European to set foot in America? For many years, people thought it was Christopher Columbus, who first crossed the Atlantic in 1492. Later, historians learned that the Vikings had settled in North America about five hundred years before Columbus. But some people think that an Irish saint might have reached North America hundreds of years before the Vikings. He was Saint Brendan, who lived during the A.D. 500s. According to a legend called *Navigatio Brendani (The Voyage of Brendan)*, he sailed to America in a wooden-and-leather boat. But many people think the story is fictitious.

In 1976 an adventurer named Tim Severin set out to see if Brendan's story might have been true. Severin built a boat just like the one Brendan was said to have used. In a treacherous transatlantic voyage, Severin and his crew reached Newfoundland, Canada, proving that Brendan's voyage might have been possible. If Brendan's story is true, then he was the first Irish American.

This illuminated manuscript from the 1200s shows Saint Brendan traveling the seas, his boat beside a whale.

Their ancestors had moved to Ireland from Scotland in the early 1600s.

Facing financial hardships at home, thousands of Scotch-Irish set out on ships to North America. They came in several waves during the 1700s, primarily between 1717 and 1775. When they reached America, the Scotch-Irish found rich natural resources, growing cities, and a chance to make a good living. Some of the immigrants were skilled businesspeople and craftspeople, who soon achieved success in their new homeland. Others became pioneers. They ventured into the Appalachian Mountains of the eastern United States, which was frontier territory in the 1700s. The mountains were home to Native American tribes and wild animals. The Scotch-Irish soon

WORDS THAT CAME TO AMERICA FROM IRELAND

Many American English words have their roots in Ireland or the Gaelic language. Here are some of them and their meanings. To listen to someone speaking Irish, visit www.inamericabooks.com for links.

- banshee (a Celtic female spirit whose wailing warns of death)
- blarney (nonsense)
- galore (plentiful)
- hubbub (uproar)
- limerick (a funny poem with a specific rhyme pattern)
- smithereens (fragments)

This early ad for Irish immigrant labor appeared in a Maryland newspaper in 1792.

THEY SAY
THERE'S BREAD
AND WORK
FOR ALL / AND
THE SUN
SHINES ALWAYS
THERE.

—A description of America, included in the poem "Lament of the Irish Emigrant," written in the mid-1800s by Helen Selina, Countess of Dufferin

earned a reputation as tough frontiersmen and Indian fighters.

A few decades later, in the early 1800s, some Irish Catholics also left for America. By then a new nation had formed in North America—the United States of America. The new nation was growing. It needed laborers to build cities, roads, and canals. With few prospects at home, small groups of Irish Catholics, just a few thousand a year, crossed the ocean to take their chances in America.

Mostly farmers in Ireland, the Irish Catholic immigrants did not have professional skills. They took whatever work they could get, often jobs that other Americans did not want at wages other Americans would not accept. Irishmen and boys took laboring jobs. They dug ditches and canals, built roads, and loaded cargo. Young Irish women became household servants and nannies. Both men and women took jobs in mills and factories. A few immigrants headed out west to farm the land.

For most Irish laborers, the hours were long, the pay was low, and the work was difficult. In the north, canal diggers stood knee-deep in chilly water. In the south, ditch diggers worked in hot, buggy swamps. Diseases such as dysentery, cholera, and malaria were common at construction sites. If workers were injured on the job, they received no pay or sick leave. They were simply out of work. But the immigrants were glad to have jobs at all and their first foothold in American society.

The Irish immigrants banded together to help one another. They formed Irish American clubs, banks, orphanages, and hospitals. Immigrants in New York founded the *Shamrock,* the first Irish American newspaper, in 1810. Other Irish immigrants opened an American branch of the Ancient Order of Hibernians (Hibernian means "Irish"), an Irish charitable society, in 1836.

Life soon improved for the immigrants. They sent letters back to Ireland, encouraging friends and family to join them in America.

This coin was made in 1986 to commemorate the founding of the Ancient Order of Hibernians in America.

IRISH NAMES

Some Irish names have become common American names. Here are a few traditional Irish names and their meanings.

Brian: strong, sincere   Neil: champion

Bridget: strength   Patrick: noble

Colleen: girl   Sean: gift of God

Erin: Ireland

YOU CAN FIND TIPS ON RESEARCHING NAMES IN YOUR FAMILY HISTORY AT WWW.INAMERICABOOKS.COM.

They told of great opportunities in the United States. For example, a farmer could easily buy one hundred acres of land in the United States—more than three times bigger than the largest farms in Ireland. A job in the United States paid as much as $1.50 a day. In Ireland, a person lucky enough to find a job would accept that amount for a week's work. The immigrants wrote of daily meals in America that a family in Ireland would see only on holidays.

Hungry for cheap labor, American businesses also enticed immigrants. They posted handbills in Irish cities, advertising thousands of jobs in America at good wages. As the encouraging news spread, the flow of immigrants increased gradually. Every year, more and more Irish said farewell to their homeland and boarded ships for America.

2 FROM IRELAND TO AMERICA

In the 1800s, Ireland was a rural nation. Most people lived in small farming villages. They generally spoke Gaelic, the language of their ancestors, along with a little English. They enjoyed simple entertainments: storytelling around the fire, singing, and dancing to fiddle music with neighbors. Families typically had many children. When these children grew up, they supported their parents in old age.

Most country people in Ireland were very poor. They lived in small cottages built of wood, stone, and sod—usually with just one room for as many as twelve family members. Most homes had dirt floors and no furniture. People slept on straw mats and sometimes shared quarters with their pigs and other livestock. They wore ragged clothing. Many had no shoes.

Urban dwellers were not much better off. Cities such as Dublin and Cork were run down and full of slums. Residents suffered from poor sanitation, outbreaks of disease, malnutrition, and inadequate health care. Unlike England, which had thriving mills, factories, banks, and other businesses, Ireland had a weak economy. It had only a few successful industries, such as linen manufacturing.

The Irish population swelled in the early 1800s. Because there were so many people, farms were subdivided into smaller and smaller plots, some smaller than an acre. Rents went higher and higher, and many families, unable to pay their landlords, were evicted from their homes. They wandered from town to town begging for food. They slept in ditches by the roadside. Many died of starvation.

Most landlords did not deal directly with their tenants. They were wealthy English and Irish Protestants, some of them politicians, who lived on big estates. Some lived in England, far away from the land they owned. Rather than interact with their tenants, landlords hired agents to collect rents, evict those who couldn't pay, and enforce other regulations. Although some landlords treated their tenants kindly, many were indifferent to the

A woman sits outside with all her belongings after being evicted from her house in County Mayo, Ireland.

suffering of the people who worked their land.

THE GREAT FAMINE

Depending on their region, Irish farmers grew many crops, such as barley, wheat, and oats. But growers dared not eat these crops, even when their families were hungry. Instead, the crops were handed over as rent to their landlords. For their own food, Irish farmers grew potatoes. Some families had a few animals—perhaps some chickens or ducks, a pig or a cow. These animals provided a little extra food: eggs, meat, milk, and butter. Along the seacoast, some people fished for cod, haddock, or herring.

But people ate mostly potatoes. They also fed potatoes to their animals. These vegetables grew in great quantities on just small plots of land. They were easy to grow and thrived in the moist Irish soil. Potatoes were a godsend for the Irish. Without potatoes, the Irish could not survive.

It was nothing short of disaster, then, when the potato crop failed in 1845. The failure was caused by disease, or blight, stemming from a fungus. When the blight hit, potato fields turned black. Potatoes rotted soon after they were dug from the ground. Racked with hunger, people

A hungry Irish family digs in the ground, looking for potatoes that haven't been damaged by blight.

sometimes ate the rotten potatoes anyway and got
sick. As the blight spread across Ireland, people
became desperate. They sold their animals, bedding,
and other possessions to buy food. They ate cabbage
leaves, raw turnips, nettles, and seaweed, even cats and
dogs. Weakened and malnourished, thousands fell sick
with diseases such as typhus and dysentery.

Famine gripped Ireland. Yet many landlords
ignored their tenants' suffering. Worried about their
own finances, landlords continued to evict families
who couldn't pay the rent. Agents tore down cottages
and ran families off the land. Starving, sick, and
homeless, thousands began to die. Soon there were
not enough able-bodied people to care for the dead
and dying.

The British government took some steps to feed
the hungry. It imported corn from the United States,
but not nearly enough to feed the starving population.
It created job programs, such as road building to
employ laborers, but these programs were ineffective.
Those given jobs were usually too weak and hungry
to work. Wages were not high enough to feed a family.
A few private organizations, such as the Quakers in
the United States, set up soup depots in Irish cities.
American charities also sent money to Ireland.

But none of these efforts were enough to stop the
devastation. Men, women, and children were reduced
to skeletons. Some moved to public institutions called
poorhouses and died there. Others died at home or
along roadsides. Many were buried in mass graves. In

FOR LINKS TO MORE
INFORMATION
ON THE GREAT FAMINE
IN IRELAND, VISIT
WWW.INAMERICABOOKS.COM.

County Mayo, one of the worst hit areas of Ireland, one out of every three people died of starvation or disease.

Historians have pointed out that Ireland actually had large amounts of food during the famine—stores of wheat, oats, and barley; and bacon, eggs, and butter—more than enough to feed its people. But this food was not given to the hungry or sold to them at low prices. Instead, it was shipped out for sale to England, Scotland, and other nations. Food was valuable merchandise. Regardless of the suffering in Ireland, landowners wanted to sell it for the best possible price.

The blight continued through 1850. By the time it was over, about one million people—roughly one-eighth of the Irish population—had died of starvation or disease. At least another 1.25 million literally "ran for their lives." They fled to America.

A SAD FAREWELL

The starving people saw no future for themselves in Ireland. Their ancient homeland held nothing but despair and suffering. But the United States seemed to offer salvation for the desperate, famine-stricken Irish. By 1846 the roads to the Irish coast bustled with activity. Families and solitary travelers pressed toward seaport towns, where they could buy tickets for passenger ships to North America.

The British government, overwhelmed by masses of starving people, encouraged the Irish to leave. It was easier to ship the hungry to America, officials reasoned,

THE FAMINE? . . . NO, THE STARVATION! WHEN A COUNTRY IS FULL OF FOOD AND EXPORTING IT, THERE CAN BE NO FAMINE.

—*George Bernard Shaw*, Man and Superman

Irish emigrants on the docks of Queenstown, Ireland, prepare to leave for New York City.

than to care for them in Ireland. What's more, Great Britain needed settlers in Canada, its sparsely populated North American colony. The government arranged for ships to carry passengers to Canada for low fares. Landlords encouraged emigration too, especially after 1847, when the government announced that landowners would be required to care for the poor on their estates. Rather than bear this cost, landlords chose to pay their tenants' passage to America.

While many Irish boarded ships for Canada, others wanted no part of the hated British Empire—England and its many colonies around the world. They wanted to live in the United States—a land of liberty and independence—free of British control. Because of stricter regulations and better ships, it cost more to travel to the United States than to Canada—more than three times the price. But tens of thousands scraped together the money for tickets. Many borrowed

In this illustration, a woman on the shores of Ireland stands on a rock that says "We are starving," while signaling for help from U.S. ships.

money from relatives who were already living in North America. Others traveled cheaply to Canada and then illegally crossed the border into the United States.

In 1847 more than one hundred thousand emigrants left Ireland for North America. That yearly figure increased steadily, reaching more than two hundred thousand in 1851. Altogether, more than five thousand emigrant ships left for North America during six years of famine. Few Irish people really wanted to leave their home country, the beautiful green land of their ancestors. But most felt they had no choice. To stay in Ireland meant almost certain death.

ACROSS THE WIDE ATLANTIC

A voyage across the Atlantic Ocean in the mid-1800s was a miserable experience. The fastest voyages took more than four weeks. But if winds were unfavorable, the trip could take ten weeks. Shipowners increased profits by cramming as many passengers as possible into tight quarters below deck. Often the immigrants were denied any comfort at all. Food supplies were meager and sometimes rotten. Toilet areas were foul smelling and filthy. Drinking water was scarce and too precious to use for bathing or washing clothes.

The passengers were hungry, dirty, and weak to begin with. Diseases such as typhus and yellow fever swept through the crowded ships. Shipboard burial services were routine, with more than one-fifth of the passengers dying during some trips. Immigrants to Canada faced the worst conditions and the most misery and disease. The worst of the Irish transports earned the nickname "coffin ships."

Still, the travelers remained positive. After all, they had experienced worse suffering in Ireland. When the ships neared land, the passengers' hope turned to excitement. They expected paradise, and the bustling harbors of North America—cities such as Boston, Massachusetts; New York City, New York; Baltimore, Maryland; New Orleans, Louisiana; and Philadelphia, Pennsylvania—gave a promising first impression.

For many immigrants, that promise would never be fulfilled. Passengers disembarked at landing points such as Deer Island

MANY PEOPLE ARE INTERESTED IN LEARNING ABOUT THEIR FAMILY'S HISTORY. THIS STUDY IS CALLED GENEALOGY. IF YOU'D LIKE TO LEARN ABOUT YOUR OWN GENEALOGY AND HOW YOUR ANCESTORS CAME TO AMERICA, VISIT WWW.INAMERICABOOKS.COM FOR TIPS AND LINKS TO HELP YOU GET STARTED.

Immigrants arrive at the docks in New York in 1850.

in Boston, Staten Island in New York, and Grosse Isle near Montreal. Sometimes, doctors boarded the ships and examined the passengers. In some cases, more than 20 percent of them carried an infectious disease. The worst of the sick were quarantined, or isolated. They were sent to "fever ships" or special hospitals, so that disease wouldn't spread among city populations. Many travelers died in quarantine or right on the docks, before ever setting foot on the American mainland. Others came onshore, hungry and penniless but full of hope. Some travelers emptied small packets of Irish soil onto the North American ground. The gesture symbolized the wedding of Ireland and America.

DIFFICULT FIRST STEPS

Immigrants walked off the boats frightened and confused, many dressed in rags. Most of them had lived in small villages in Ireland, and they were overwhelmed by America's big port cities. A number of travelers were children, sent alone to live with relatives who had already come to America. Most immigrants knew some English, which was spoken along with Gaelic in their home country. But they knew virtually nothing about the United States or city life. They were easy marks for runners, or con artists, many of them Irish Americans who had arrived years earlier. Pretending to be helpful and speaking with familiar Irish accents, the runners greeted immigrants right off the ship. Using all sorts of tricks, the runners sometimes stole immigrants' money, sold them phony train tickets, or led them to overpriced lodging houses.

Eventually, government officials stepped in to assist the travelers. In 1855 New York City established the nation's first immigration station, a building called Castle Garden. There, newcomers were temporarily

Agents at Castle Garden in New York City helped Irish immigrants get their bearings in their new home.

safe from runners, pickpockets, and other cheats. Immigration officials gave travelers advice and assisted children traveling alone to meet relatives. Immigrants could buy food, train tickets, and lodging at the station at fair prices.

But soon the immigrants were on their own. Most settled in the cities where they had landed. They usually had no choice. Most were penniless when they got off the boats, so they took whatever housing they could find nearby, no matter how run down. They packed into tenement apartments with other Irish immigrants. Large families commonly lived in just one room. Many dwellings lacked light, fresh air, and running water. Outhouses overflowed, and sewage seeped into the streets. Garbage was put outside to decay and rot. Drinking water was often polluted.

FOR LINKS TO MORE INFORMATION ON HOW IRISH IMMIGRANTS ADJUSTED TO LIFE IN THE UNITED STATES, VISIT WWW.INAMERICABOOKS.COM.

In such conditions, disease was quick to spread. In 1849 a cholera epidemic spread along the East Coast of the United States. More than five hundred of the seven hundred people who died were Irish. A yellow fever epidemic raged through New Orleans in 1853, killing about 20 percent of the Irish immigrants there.

GAINING GROUND

Although most Irish immigrants stayed in America's port cities, others ventured west. In the mid–1800s, land was cheap and plentiful in the nation's interior, and many immigrants moved there to start farms. They established towns such as Dublin, Ohio, and

Many Irishmen who came to the United States without families found work and excitement out west. These men work on the Northern Pacific Railroad in Dakota Territory.

Belfast, Pennsylvania, named for their old homes in Ireland. Others moved to big midwestern cities such as Saint Louis, Missouri, and Saint Paul, Minnesota. Chicago, Illinois, was a popular destination, and a huge Irish American community developed there. Some immigrants went farther west—some of them all the way to San Francisco, California.

Young single men headed west to mine gold in California or to take jobs with the railroad. Laborers were in high demand out west. To recruit workers, railroads and construction companies advertised in the newspapers of eastern cities. They also kept advertising in Ireland, enticing more and more to immigrate, first across the ocean and then across North America.

"PADDY WORKS ON THE RAILWAY"

Laying railroad track, a common job for immigrant Irishmen, was dangerous work. To build railroads across the American frontier, laborers had to blast tunnels through rock and rugged terrain. Accidents and cave-ins caused many deaths on the job. A popular saying claimed that an Irishman was buried under every American railroad tie.

Railroad workers had to blast passageways through mountainous terrain. Working with explosives was always a dangerous venture.

IRISHWOMEN IN THE WORKFORCE

Upon arrival in the United States, many unmarried Irishwomen entered domestic service. They became live-in cooks, nannies, and maids in the homes of upper-class Americans. These jobs were considered good ones. They offered a steady paycheck, housing, and a comfortable workplace for young women who had known nothing but poverty and hunger in Ireland. Many Irish servant women sent much of their salaries back to Ireland to support their families left behind or to pay relatives' passage to America.

Other immigrant Irishwomen worked in mills and factories. Once the Irish had become more established in the United States, Irishwomen began to enter skilled professions. They often became nuns, nurses, and teachers.

[AL]THOUGH I AM IN A STRANGE COUNTRY, I AM NOT AMONG STRANGE PEOPLE.

—*Irish immigrant Samuel Laird, 1850*

But most immigrants stayed in the eastern cities. All along the East Coast, the Irish population continued to swell. Immigrants kept flooding in, with thirty thousand arriving in Boston in 1847 alone. By 1850 New York City had more Irish people than Dublin, the biggest city in Ireland.

Often, people from the same town or city in Ireland congregated in a certain part of New York or Boston. A neighborhood nicknamed Corktown, for example, would be filled with people from Cork, Ireland. Early on, Boston's North End and Greenwich

Village in New York became thriving "Irish towns"—rich with the language, music, and customs of Ireland.

In Ireland the Roman Catholic Church had been the center of community life. The same was true in the United States. At first, Irish immigrants could not afford to build big churches. But once their communities became established and church members had achieved some success, people pitched in to build grand cathedrals. Old Saint Patrick's in Chicago (1856) and Saint Patrick's in New York (1858) are some of the finest examples. These elaborate structures boast intricate stained-glass windows and ornate statues. Such churches offered Irish Catholics an important spiritual headquarters. They also served as community centers. Priests not only led religious worship, they were also important leaders in Irish American neighborhoods.

The immigrants also formed clubs such as the Friendly Sons of Saint Patrick, Saint Patrick's Mutual Alliance, and the Legion of Mary. These groups undertook charity work as well as social activities, such as organizing Saint Patrick's Day parades. Some groups, such as the Hibernian Society for the Relief of Emigrants and the Irish Emigrant Society, focused

The elegant Saint Patrick's Cathedral stands tall in New York City.

solely on helping newcomers adjust to life in the United States. The Emigrant Industrial Savings Bank, opened in New York in 1850, gave Irish New Yorkers a way to save and borrow money. The Ancient Order of Hibernians (AOH), the most prominent Irish society, grew with the Irish American community, gradually spreading westward across the United States.

THE ANGLO-AMERICAN BACKLASH

In coming to the United States, the Irish were not all that different from those who had arrived earlier. In fact, the United States had been founded by immigrants. It had been settled primarily by English and Dutch colonists, as well as their African American slaves. Later, Germans, Scottish, Scotch–Irish, Scandinavians, French, and other groups arrived in

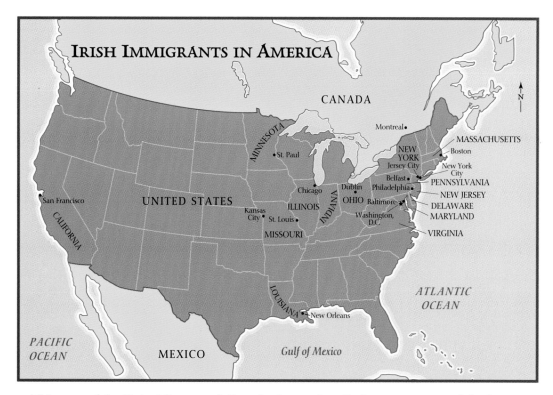

This map of the United States and Canada shows where Irish immigrants settled when they first came to their new land. To download this map, visit www.inamericabooks.com.

the United States. These early immigrants came in fairly small numbers. They were soon integrated into mainstream American society.

But the Irish famine immigrants came in very large numbers. In 1840, five years before the famine, about 84,000 immigrants arrived in the United States from many different countries around the world. In 1850, the last year of the famine, the total number of immigrants was 370,000—more than half of them Irish. Even after 1850, when the potato crop recovered and the famine ended, the Irish continued to arrive in America—as many as 50,000 per year.

Although the United States had encouraged immigration, largely to get cheap laborers, many Americans were upset when masses of starving Irish people began to arrive in their cities. By American standards, the immigrants were uneducated and poorly clothed. Their neighborhoods were crowded and dirty. Their manners and language were coarse. They fought and got drunk and slacked off at work, the Americans said. To many Americans, worst of all was that the Irish immigrants were Roman Catholics. Most Americans were Protestant, primarily of English descent. These Anglo- (English-) Americans disapproved of Catholicism, just as their ancestors had in England.

Many Americans, although descendants of immigrants themselves, resented the Irish. This cartoon from the 1800s shows a "Poor House from Galway" carrying Ireland's poor to America. For links to more information on anti-Irish sentiment in the United States, visit www.inamericabooks.com.

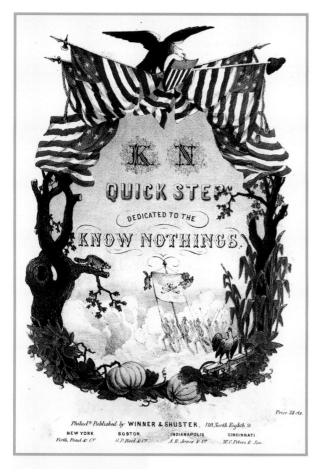

The Know-Nothings became an extremely powerful political party in the mid-1800s. The sheet music pictured above was dedicated to the group.

As the numbers of Irish immigrants grew, anti-Catholic and anti-Irish feelings swept through the United States. Irish immigrants were ridiculed and abused. Some employers refused to hire them. In a few cases, Catholic churches were attacked. Anglo-Americans were especially worried about Catholic political power, which was growing in several cities. In response, one group formed the Know-Nothing Party, officially named the American Party. Created in 1852, this political party opposed immigration and the election or appointment of Catholics to government posts. Meetings were held in secret, and the party earned its nickname because members replied "I don't know" to questions about the group's activities. The Know-Nothings put dozens of candidates into state and national office—governors, senators, and representatives. The party even nominated a candidate for president in 1856, but he did poorly in the election. Soon the party split over the question of slavery, and the Know-Nothings then faded from the political scene.

3

THE IRISH AMERICAN DREAM

The Civil War—the War between the States—broke out in the United States in 1861. The war primarily concerned slavery, which had been abolished in the North but was legal in the South. Rather than free the African American slaves who worked their farms and plantations, eleven Southern states broke from the United States (the Union) and formed the Confederate States of America. President Abraham Lincoln called the Northern states to arms to save the Union.

The Irish had primarily settled in the North. Their old oppressors, the British, supported the Confederate states, which supplied Great Britain with cotton. It seemed natural, then, that the Irish would back the Northern cause. But, in fact, many Irish were halfhearted about the war to end slavery. Some saw little difference between the suffering of black slaves in the South and their own hardships in the North. They endured so much misery in the slums of New York and Boston that many felt indifferent to the troubles of African Americans. Others were hostile to African Americans—they feared that freed blacks, willing to work for even less than the Irish, would take jobs from Irish workers.

Despite mixed feelings, when President Lincoln called for volunteers to join the Union army, many Irishmen responded. The army offered a paycheck, after all, and many immigrants needed a job. Others were eager to prove their allegiance to their newly adopted nation. The number of Irishmen in the Union army has been estimated at 150,000 to 170,000. Irishmen joined the Confederacy as well,

Irish American troops of the Union's Ninth Massachusetts Infantry get ready for a church service while stationed in Virginia in 1861.

Irish general Meagher leads his Union troops into battle at Fair Oaks, Virginia, on June 1, 1862.

although their numbers were smaller because fewer Irish had settled in the South.

Early in the war, an Irish officer named Thomas Meagher organized an all–Irish force: the Irish Brigade. Part of the Army of the Potomac, the brigade was made up of four New York regiments, plus one from Pennsylvania and another from Massachusetts. Each regiment carried a green flag, decorated with symbols of Ireland such as the shamrock and the harp. Under Meagher's command, the brigade fought bravely for the Union in many important battles, including those at Gettysburg, Pennsylvania; Fredericksburg, Virginia; Chancellorsville, Virginia; and Antietam, Maryland.

FOR LINKS TO MORE INFORMATION ABOUT IRISH AMERICAN TROOPS IN THE CIVIL WAR, VISIT WWW.INAMERICABOOKS.COM.

> *Says Pat to his mother,*
> *it looks strange to see /*
> *Brothers fighting in such*
> *a queer manner, /*
> *But I'll fight till I die and*
> *I'll surely be killed /*
> *For America's bright starry*
> *banner.*
>
> —*"Pat Murphy of the Irish*
> *Brigade," Civil War song*

"ENOUGH OF YOUR HARD FIGHTING"

Back in New York, however, the Irish community was growing angry with the U.S. government. Many Irish opposed Abraham Lincoln's Emancipation Proclamation, made in 1863, which freed all African Americans in Confederate states. Hostility toward African Americans increased further when blacks were hired to break an Irish dockworkers' strike. Then, with the Union suffering heavy losses, the U.S. government passed a law to draft additional men into

the army through a lottery system. This action inflamed Irish New Yorkers. The law allowed a man to hire a replacement for three hundred dollars to serve in the army for him. Most Irishmen were laborers who could not afford a replacement. They had no choice but to serve if they were drafted, while the rich could simply buy their way out of service.

The first New York draft lottery, held on July 11, 1863, produced a list of twelve hundred names—the majority of them Irish. Following publication of the list, angry Irish workers gathered at draft centers and vacant lots. When the New York Police Department attempted to break up the crowds, the workers attacked. Police superintendent John Kennedy, himself an Irishman, was badly beaten. The rioting continued for four days. Large Irish mobs roamed the city, attacking a military depot on Lexington Avenue and the homes of merchants and community leaders. But the rioters' main targets were African Americans. An orphanage for black

children was burned, many blacks were beaten, and others were hanged. By the time U.S. troops moved in to end the rioting, hundreds of people had been injured and more than fifty killed. Of the thousands of rioters, several hundred were arrested. But only a handful of them were convicted of crimes.

"UNION MEN BE STRONG"

When the Civil War ended, Irish Americans went back to work—in factories and mills, on farms, and on the railroads. It was a time of great growth in the United States. Big cities filled up with shops, streetcars, and skyscrapers. Roads, railroads, and bridges linked cities and towns from coast to coast. Keeping it all moving were the workers—the people who dug the coal that fueled the factories, manufactured the steel bridges and railroad tracks, and built the tall buildings in cities such as New York and Chicago. A great number of these workers were Irish.

At many jobs, Irish laborers endured brutal working conditions. Some worked twelve hours a day, six days a week for rock–bottom wages. Employers sometimes cheated and abused their workers. In many cases, even children were employed in dangerous mines and factories. There were few laws to protect anyone on the job.

The coal mines of western Pennsylvania, which employed many Irish laborers, offered some of the most dangerous working

TERROR TACTICS

In the 1860s and 1870s, a group of Irish miners in western Pennsylvania, members of a secret society called the Molly Maguires, struck back violently against mining companies that treated workers cruelly. The Mollies terrorized coal mine bosses with threats, beatings, and killings. Eventually, mine owners gained access to the organization, and the Mollies were brought down. In 1877 nineteen Molly Maguires were hanged for crimes against the coal bosses.

A meeting of the Molly McGuires in 1874

conditions in the country. Mine cave–ins were common. Poisonous gases sometimes seeped into mines and killed many workers. At most mines, workers' lives were completely controlled by the mining company. The company supplied miners and their families with housing, food, and equipment, often at greatly inflated prices. Many miners fell deeply in debt to the company. They were frequently cheated out of a fair day's pay.

By the late 1800s, American laborers had had enough of such treatment. They wanted safe working conditions and fair wages. They wanted laws to protect workers on the job, especially children. They wanted unions that could bargain with employers over issues such as pay, time off, and job safety. All

These Irish pipe layers were employed by Standard Oil in the late 1890s.

In the late 1800s and early 1900s, some Irish boys had dangerous jobs working in mines. The boys shown here worked in Pennsylvania in 1911.

across the nation, laborers began to form construction, factory, and mining unions. They joined prominent national groups such as the Knights of Labor and the American Federation of Labor. Irish Americans were at the forefront of this movement.

Terence Powderly, the son of Irish immigrants, had taken the top position with the Knights of Labor in 1879. Under his leadership, the organization grew large and powerful. Mary Harris "Mother" Jones, born in Cork, Ireland, was another union pioneer. She led coal miner strikes, fought to protect child workers, and helped found the Industrial Workers of the World (IWW), a radical labor organization. Elizabeth Gurley Flynn, also a child of Irish immigrants, led many IWW

Mother Jones was a strong fighter for workers' rights. Here she marches for miners' rights in Trinidad, Colorado, in 1913.

strikes. She is remembered in song as "The Union Maid." Ultimately, after many bloody battles, unions won great gains for American workers—Irish and non–Irish alike.

THE ROAD TO SUCCESS

Even in the early 1900s, Irish immigrants continued to arrive in the United States. But their numbers were by then dwarfed by newer waves of immigrant groups. Germans, Scandinavians, Poles, Italians, and Jews and other Eastern Europeans settled on the East Coast. Chinese, Japanese, and other Asians arrived on the West Coast. It was their turn to struggle for a foothold in American society—to crowd into ramshackle tenements and take dangerous jobs for low pay.

FOR LINKS TO MORE ABOUT THE IRISH IMMIGRANT LABOR EXPERIENCE, VISIT WWW.INAMERICABOOKS.COM.

The McGovern family of Philadelphia poses in front of their new flag in the early 1900s.

The Irish were no longer newcomers to America. They had learned about American ways and customs. They had fought for the nation bravely in the Civil War, and they had raised children and even grandchildren in their new homeland. Viewing themselves as fully American, the Irish were eager to leave the immigrant experience behind. Their children identified with the United States, not Ireland. Although many Irish still labored in low–paying jobs, others entered skilled professions. Large numbers found work as firefighters and police officers. Many opened stores, factories, and other kinds of businesses. Some grew wealthy.

IRISH FIREFIGHTERS: THEN AND NOW

In the late 1800s, large numbers of Irish immigrants, especially in New York and Boston, became firefighters. New York City created a fire department in 1865, and most of its first fire commissioners and fire chiefs were Irish. Throughout the 1900s,

firefighting remained a popular profession for Irish Americans. It's no surprise that when the New York Fire Department rushed into the World Trade Center after the terrorist attacks on September 11, 2001, many of the heroic firefighters there were Irish Americans. Almost 350 firefighters died in the Twin Towers that day. About 25 percent of them had Irish last names.

"America for the Americans"

Each new immigrant group faced discrimination in the United States, just as the Irish had when they first arrived. The newcomers were ridiculed for their unfamiliar accents, religious practices, and foreign dress. On the West Coast, one trade organization lashed out against Chinese immigrants, who took jobs from other laborers by working for very low wages. Members recited slogans such as "the Chinese must go" and "America for the Americans." Ironically, the group's leader, Dennis Kearney, had been born in Ireland.

Education was important to the Irish. It offered a promising path to success. But most American schools had a Protestant bias. Children there learned about Protestant culture and read from the King James, or Protestant, Bible. Many Irish American parents wanted their children to have a Catholic education. So they built parochial, or religious, schools to teach their children both academics and Catholic studies. Generations of Irish American children attended these schools.

At the university level, the Irish found that many schools would not admit Catholics or had strict limits on Catholic admission. So, many Irish Americans enrolled in Jesuit universities and colleges, which had been founded by Jesuit priests. Jesuits are members of the Roman Catholic Society of Jesus founded by St. Ignatius Loyola. Jesuits are devoted to humanitarian and

Fordham University was founded in New York by a group of Jesuits who came from Kentucky. The majority of the 28 Jesuits who made the trip to New York were French. One American-born and four Irish-born Jesuits were among them.

educational work. Jesuit schools include Fordham University in New York, Loyola University in Chicago, Catholic University in Washington, D.C., and Boston College in Boston. Founded by French priests, the University of Notre Dame in Indiana attracted many Irish students—so many that the school's athletic teams soon earned the nickname the Fighting Irish. As more and more Irish Americans earned college degrees, they began to enter skilled professions such as teaching, medicine, engineering, and law.

POLITICAL MIGHT

As the numbers of Irish grew in big cities such as Boston, Chicago, and New York, so did Irish political power. Irish politicians generally organized at the neighborhood level, taking control of precincts, or local voting districts. Often, political meetings were held in the local saloon. Irish Americans soon became city councillors and mayors. They gained considerable power in the city halls of New York, Boston, and other cities.

Irish politicians were effective but not always ethical. To win votes for preferred candidates, Irish precinct captains sometimes bribed voters, especially new immigrants. In exchange for votes, precinct captains helped immigrants get jobs and social services—sometimes even paid them. In New York, a Democratic organization called Tammany Hall used such tactics to gain and maintain power. Strong and well organized, this network was called a "machine." Its leaders were called "bosses." Many of them were Irish. Tammany Hall, particularly in the late 1800s, had a reputation for greed and corruption. Some bosses ran illegal businesses such as gambling and prostitution rings. Police were paid to "look the other way."

Tammany Hall workers approach voters at the polls. Some Irish politicians used dishonest tactics to win votes.

But despite its reputation for corruption, Tammany Hall was actually an effective political group with strong local support. Many poor Irish immigrants were able to rise through its ranks to high government offices. The most famous was Alfred E. Smith, who moved up from Tammany into New York state government, becoming governor in 1919. In this job, which he held for four terms,

Supporters of Alfred E. Smith for president display signs during the Democratic National Convention in Chicago in 1928.

Smith championed the rights of workers and immigrants. In 1928 he ran for president, the first Irish Catholic to do so. But many Protestant Americans, particularly in small towns out west, were suspicious of Smith, a big-city Irish man—and a Catholic. In part because of anti-Catholic feelings, Smith lost the election to Republican Herbert Hoover.

Smith's defeat did little to weaken Irish political power. Throughout the 1900s, Irish American mayors ran America's big cities: Jimmy Walker in New York, James Curley in Boston, Richard J. Daley in Chicago, Thomas Pendergast in Kansas City, Missouri, and Frank Hague in Jersey City, New Jersey. Other Irish Americans held state and national offices, serving as governors,

NEW YORK IS A GRAND HANDSOME CITY. BUT YOU WOULD HARDLY KNOW YOU HAD LEFT IRELAND, THERE ARE SO MANY IRISH PEOPLE HERE. SOME OF THEM ARE RICH. SOME OF THEM ARE BIG MEN IN GOVERNMENT.

—immigrant Patrick Murphy, late 1800s

congressional representatives, and Supreme Court justices.

MELTED INTO THE POT

Throughout the mid–1900s, Irish Americans clung tightly to their ethnic identity. They lived in primarily Irish neighborhoods. They generally married other Irish Catholics. They maintained strong ties to the Church, often sending their children to Catholic schools.

But after World War II (1939–1945), the Irish community began to splinter. By then many Irish Americans had achieved clear-cut success. They were members of the middle class—in some cases the upper class. Like many other white Americans, the Irish moved out of the nation's crowded urban centers after the war. They left their old Irish neighborhoods for the suburbs of Boston, Chicago, Philadelphia, and other big cities. These newly built communities often held a mix of ethnic groups such as Irish, Germans, Poles, and Italians; and Catholics, Protestants, and Jews. The old "Irish towns" began to fade away.

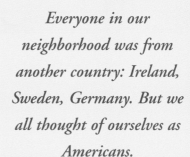

Everyone in our neighborhood was from another country: Ireland, Sweden, Germany. But we all thought of ourselves as Americans.

—Tom Collins Sr., the son of Irish immigrants who came to Chicago in 1905

The Irish community was changing, but it was certainly not gone. Irish Americans still took great pride in their heritage, especially in 1960, when John F. Kennedy was elected president of the United States. Kennedy was the first Irish Catholic to hold this office. Even in the 1960s, though, more than one hundred years after the famine immigration, some Anglo-Americans didn't like the idea of a Catholic president. But with Kennedy's victory, the last barrier to Irish achievement had fallen: an Irish Catholic had reached the highest office in the land.

IRISH AMERICAN DYNASTY

When it comes to politics, one Irish name stands out above all others: Kennedy. Boston's Joseph P. Kennedy was the grandson of a penniless Irish immigrant. He built up a great fortune as an investment banker and used it to advance the political careers of his sons. The most famous son, John F. Kennedy, became president of the United States in 1961. He was assassinated in 1963. Robert Kennedy, the third son, served as attorney general during his brother's administration. He too was assassinated, while campaigning

Joseph Kennedy (center in glasses) *and family, including John* (back row left) *and Robert* (front row, left), *have fun at the beach.*

Right: *President John F. Kennedy.*
Below: *Robert Kennedy* (center)
campaigns for U.S. Senate in New
York City in 1964 with his sons (from
left to right) *Robert Jr., David, and*
Joseph II.

for the U.S. presidency in 1968. The youngest son, Edward (Ted),
has served in the U.S. Senate since 1962.

Some members of the third generation also entered politics.
For example, Joseph Kennedy II, Robert's second child, served as
a congressman from Boston from 1987 to 1999. Kathleen
Kennedy Townsend, Robert's oldest child, was lieutenant gover-
nor of Maryland from 1995 to 2003. Maria Shriver, Eunice
Kennedy Shriver's daughter, is married to Arnold
Schwarzenegger, who was elected governor of California in
2003.

TROUBLE IN IRELAND

The Irish had fared well in the United States. Back in Ireland, however, the people still struggled for freedom. After a long series of conflicts and negotiations with the British government, the mostly Catholic southern counties of Ireland had finally won independence in 1949. The heavily Protestant northern counties remained part of the United Kingdom, with strong political ties to England. Thus the island became two countries: the Republic of Ireland in the south (mostly Catholic) and small Northern Ireland in the northeast (about half Protestant).

In Belfast, Northern Ireland, students in 1968 protest unfair treatment by the British-controlled government.

But old hatreds still simmered. In the late 1960s, Catholics in Northern Ireland demonstrated against

When British authorities tried to control demonstrations, some protests turned violent, such as this one in Londonderry, Northern Ireland, in 1969.

the British/Protestant–controlled government there. Catholics charged that they were discriminated against in the areas of housing, jobs, education, and voting rights. When the government tried to shut down the demonstrations, rioting broke out. Some militant Catholic groups struck out at Protestant citizens and British authorities with bombings, kidnappings, and other terrorist acts. Known as the Troubles, the violence dragged on through the rest of the century.

Many were killed in the fighting.

To make matters worse, the Irish economy had never been strong. Unemployment was widespread. Young people graduating from high school and college saw few job prospects awaiting them in Ireland. The violence in the north only worsened people's despair. So like their ancestors a century before them, many Irish began to leave their nation. A large migration occurred in the late 1980s. The immigrants were mostly young and well educated. They took jobs in many countries, including England, Australia, and South Africa. Many people went to the United States.

The new Irish immigrants to the United States had a very different experience than the starving travelers of the mid–1800s. They traveled to the United States by airplane instead of boat. Unlike the first wave of Irish immigrants, they were generally welcomed warmly and easily adapted to American life and culture. They took jobs in a variety of fields and professions.

Some of the "new Irish" took formal steps to apply for U.S. citizenship. Others applied for permission to work and live in the United States but did not become citizens. Still other Irish immigrants did not follow the law. They arrived on tourist visas, documents that allowed them to visit the United States for only a short time. Then they stayed in the country illegally, living and working without the knowledge or permission of the U.S. government. Thanks to changes in U.S. immigration law in the 1980s and 1990s, many of these "illegals" have since been granted citizenship. The Irish Centre for Migration Studies estimates that approximately 220,000 recent Irish–born immigrants are living in the United States.

"KISS ME, I'M IRISH"

By the time the new Irish started to arrive in the late 1900s, the old Irish Americans had largely lost touch with their roots. The first–generation immigrants were all but gone. Few people remembered Ireland and the suffering of their ancestors. Few remembered the songs, folktales, and traditional language of Ireland.

A young Irish boy celebrates his heritage during the Irish Fest in Milwaukee, Wisconsin.

What's more, some Irish Americans had parted with the Catholic community by then. Some had married Protestants or people of other faiths. Others had quit the Church. For some Irish Americans, their only connection to their heritage was a last name like Sullivan, Murphy, or Griffin.

But then the tide turned again. In the last few decades of the 1900s, people of all ethnic backgrounds began to search for their roots. Irish Americans were no exception. Although the famine immigrants had long since passed away, their great- and great-great-grandchildren wanted to reclaim their Irish heritage. They began an Irish revival that continues into the 2000s.

In the modern United States, people of all backgrounds have embraced Irish culture. Many Americans love Irish fiddle music and folk songs. They tune into National Public Radio's *Thistle and Shamrock*, a long-running show featuring the best of traditional Irish (as well as Scottish) music. In big cities across the United States, people gather at Irish-style pubs. Some people enjoy watching or learning how to step dance, a traditional Irish-style dance. Others attend Irish festivals, yearly celebrations filled with Irish music, dance, food, and traditions. Some people have become fascinated with ancient Celtic culture and religion. A few even study Gaelic, the original Celtic language. Others enjoy modern Irish culture, including contemporary Irish performers such as U2 and Enya.

FOR LINKS TO MORE INFORMATION ABOUT TRADITIONAL AND CONTEMPORARY IRISH CULTURE, VISIT WWW.INAMERICABOOKS.COM.

In the search for their roots, many Irish Americans try to trace their family trees back to Ireland. They study ships' logs, old newspapers, and other records to find out when and where their ancestors arrived in the United States. Others visit Ireland, especially the hometowns of their ancestors. All this attention has helped Ireland. Its tourism industry is thriving—part of a larger and much-heralded economic recovery of the 1990s and early 2000s.

Popular Irish band U2 performs a concert.

CORNED BEEF AND CABBAGE

Corned beef and cabbage has been an Irish American favorite since the first large wave of Irish came to the United States. For a taste of other Irish recipes, visit www.inamericabooks.com.

1 TBSP. VEGETABLE OIL

1 LARGE WHITE ONION, CUT INTO RINGS

1 CLOVE GARLIC, PEELED AND MINCED

2 POUNDS PACKAGED CORNED BEEF, PICKLED IN READY-MADE BRINE

1 TSP. SALT

½ TSP. PEPPER

1 BAY LEAF

1 TSP. MUSTARD SEEDS OR PICKLING SPICE

1 SMALL HEAD GREEN CABBAGE WASHED, CORED, AND CUT INTO QUARTERS

1. Heat oil in a large pot over medium heat. Sauté onion and garlic in oil until onion is golden brown. Reduce heat to low.
2. Remove corned beef from package and rinse with cold water. Blot excess water with a paper towel.
3. Using a wooden spoon, push onions and garlic to one side of pot. Place corned beef, fatty side down, in the middle of the pot. Turn heat up to medium-high. Cook for 5 minutes to brown, turn meat over and brown for 5 more minutes.
4. Add salt, pepper, bay leaf, mustard seeds, and water to just cover meat. Turn heat to medium-low, cover, and simmer for 2½ hours.
5. Remove cover and add cabbage. Replace cover and simmer for 20 minutes. Remove from heat.
6. Remove corned beef to a large serving plate and slice into medium-sized pieces. Remove cabbage with a slotted spoon and arrange around sliced corned beef before serving.

Serves 4

On March 17 each year, Irish Americans come together to show their colors—mostly green, the color of the Emerald Isle. Across the United States, cities large and small hold Saint Patrick's Day parades. Naturally, the Irish American strongholds of New York, Chicago, and Boston have the biggest parades in the country. People of many different backgrounds enjoy the celebrations. But Irish Americans are the stars of the show. They wear green clothing, play Irish tunes, and sport buttons that say "Kiss Me, I'm Irish."

It's easy for modern–day Irish Americans to stay in touch with their heritage. Newspapers like the *Boston Irish Reporter*, the *Irish Echo*, and the *Irish Voice* feature news about Ireland and issues of

The Saint Patrick's Day parade in Chicago draws thousands of spectators each year.

For links to more Irish American celebrations, visit www.inamericabooks.com.

concern to Irish Americans. Many of the newspapers publish online as well as paper editions. Hundreds of websites also offer information, news, and links for the Irish American community. Americans who want to learn more about the Irish American experience can tour the Irish Heritage Trail in Boston or visit the moving Irish Hunger Memorial in New York. Those who like to cook can make traditional Irish dishes, such as corned beef and cabbage, Irish soda bread, and Irish potato cakes. A 2003 movie, *In America*, tells a heartwarming story about a modern-day Irish family moving to New York—showing that the Irish American journey continues.

Irish Americans have come far—from the blighted potato fields of Ireland to the top spots in U.S. politics, sports, business, and the arts. In one immigration song, a young man tells his sweetheart that he must leave Ireland: "The land of our forefathers we were forced to give [up]," he laments. "Now we're sailing on the ocean, for honor and promotion."

The young traveler explains that he'll send for his girlfriend after he's made his fortune in the United States. "I'm going to a foreign nation to purchase a plantation, to comfort us hereafter, all in America," he promises. For many Irish immigrants—and certainly for their descendants—that promise of honor, promotion, and fortune in the United States was indeed fulfilled.

FAMOUS IRISH AMERICANS

MATHEW BRADY (1823?–1896)

Born in northern New York to Irish immigrants, Brady was one of the world's first and most famous photographers. He is best known for his images of the Civil War: soldiers, battlefields, equipment, and military life. Although Brady made his own photographs at first, he later hired assistants to take pictures for him. Most of Brady's Civil War photographs were taken by his assistants.

GEORGE CLOONEY (b. 1961)

Born in Lexington, Kentucky, actor George Clooney grew up in a show business family. His father, Nick Clooney, aunt Rosemary Clooney, and uncle José Ferrer were all entertainers. Clooney made his own fame on the hit television show *ER*. He then went on to star in Hollywood movies, including *Batman and Robin, Three Kings, O Brother, Where Art Thou?, The Perfect Storm*, and *Intolerable Cruelty*.

RICHARD M. DALEY (b. 1942)

Chicago–born Daley is the eldest son of Richard J. Daley, a powerful politician who served as mayor of Chicago from 1955 to 1976. The younger Daley attended DePaul University in Chicago, earning both his undergraduate and law degree from the school. Following his father into politics, Daley served in the Illinois state senate from 1972 to 1980. He worked as state's attorney for Cook County (which includes Chicago) from 1980 to 1988. Again following his father, he was elected mayor of Chicago in 1989 and has been reelected three times.

F. SCOTT FITZGERALD

(1896–1940) Born in St. Paul, Minnesota, Francis Scott Key Fitzgerald went on to become one of the nation's most acclaimed writers.

He primarily wrote novels and short stories. Most of them deal with the lives of wealthy Americans during the 1920s. *The Great Gatsby* is Fitzgerald's most famous work.

MICHAEL FLATLEY (b. 1958)

Chicago-born Michael Flatley is the son of Irish immigrants. An accomplished Irish step dancer, he first learned the art from his mother and grandmother. He later took formal lessons and opened his own dance school. He also mastered traditional Irish flute playing. After touring with other dance companies, he launched his own Irish dance production, *Lord of the Dance*, in 1996.

HENRY FORD (1863–1947)

The son of an Irish immigrant, Henry Ford was born near Detroit, Michigan. He began his career as a machinist and engineer. He learned to build gasoline engines and automobiles and in 1903 founded the Ford Motor Company. Ford's company pioneered the assembly-line technique, which revolutionized automobile production. One hundred years later, Ford is still a leading American automaker.

GENE KELLY (1912–1996)

Born in Pittsburgh, Pennsylvania, Gene Kelly was one of the most popular entertainers of the mid-1900s. Dancing was his specialty. He also sang, acted, choreographed, and directed. Kelly appeared in Broadway shows and the movies. *On the Town, An American in Paris*, and *Singin' in the Rain* are among his most famous films.

GRACE KELLY (1929–1982)

Philadelphia-born Grace Kelly was a glamorous American actress turned princess. She acted mainly in the 1950s, starring in such feature films as *High Noon, Rear Window, Dial M for Murder*, and *To Catch a Thief*. In 1956 she married Prince Rainier of

Monaco. She quit acting, moved to Monaco, and had three children. But as a princess, she remained in the public spot–light until her death in a car crash in 1982.

CAROLINE KENNEDY (b. 1957)

The daughter of President John F. Kennedy, Caroline Kennedy is a lawyer who has written several books, including *In Our Defense: The Bill of Rights in Action* (1990) and *The Right to Privacy* (1995). In 1989 Kennedy and her family founded the Profiles in Courage Awards, given annually to politicians who perform selfless public service. Her most recent book, *Profiles in Courage for Our Time* (2002), examines the award winners and their work.

JOHN MADDEN (b. 1936)

Born in Austin, Minnesota, broadcaster John Madden is a famous figure in American football. He began his career as a guard for the Philadelphia Eagles. He later coached the Oakland Raiders. After retiring from coaching, Madden became a commentator for televised football games. He is known for his witty, colorful remarks, and he has won many awards for sports broadcasting. In 2002 Madden became a commentator on the popular *Monday Night Football* television program.

JOHN MCCAIN (b. 1936)

The son and grandson of navy admirals, John McCain is a leading Republican in the U.S. Senate. McCain served as a pilot during the Vietnam War. His

plane was shot down during the conflict, and he was held as a prisoner of war for more than five years. He became a congressman from Arizona in 1982 and a senator in 1985. McCain sought the Republican nomination for president in 1999 but did not receive his party's nomination.

FRANK MCCOURT (b. 1931)

Pulitzer Prize–winning writer Frank McCourt was born in Brooklyn but grew up in Limerick, Ireland. He returned to the United States at age nineteen, eventually becoming a schoolteacher. After retiring from teaching, McCourt wrote *Angela's Ashes*, the story of his childhood in Ireland. The book became an immediate best–seller and multiple award winner. McCourt's second book, *'Tis: A Memoir*, tells of his life in the United States.

MARK MCGWIRE (b. 1963)

Known as Big Mac, baseball player Mark McGwire made headlines in 1998 when he broke Roger Maris's thirty–seven–year–old season home–run record. Playing for the Saint Louis Cardinals, McGwire hit seventy home runs that season, breaking Maris's mark of sixty–one. A native of California, McGwire played for the University of Southern California, the U.S. Olympic baseball team, and the Oakland Athletics before joining the Cardinals in 1997.

MICK MOLONEY (b. 1944)

Born in Limerick, Ireland, Mick Moloney has been a leader in the folk music revival in both Ireland and the United States. As a young man in Ireland, Moloney tape–recorded the folk songs and fiddle tunes of ordinary people. A gifted singer and instrumentalist, he performed this music with a number of bands in Ireland and England. In 1973 he immigrated to the United States to study folklore at the University of Pennsylvania. Since then Moloney has performed on or produced more than fifty records. He has organized several Irish American bands and has been involved in many educational projects involving Irish music and the Irish American experience.

BILL MURRAY (b. 1950)

Born in Wilmette, Illinois, Murray is one of nine children in an Irish American family. As a child, he attended an all–boy's Catholic school. He enrolled in Regis College in Denver, Colorado, but never finished his degree. A gifted comedian, he became a member of Chicago's Second City comedy troupe, then joined the *Saturday Night Live* TV program in 1977. He went on to star in a number of film comedies, including *Caddyshack, Ghostbusters*, and *Groundhog Day.* In 2003 Murray appeared in *Lost in Translation*, a film about an American actor stuck in Japan. He received an Academy Award nomination for Best Actor for his work in the film.

SANDRA DAY O'CONNOR

(b. 1930) Born in El Paso, Texas, O'Connor is the first woman to serve on the U.S. Supreme Court. Before her appointment, she served as an assistant attorney general, a U.S. senator, and an appeals court judge in Arizona. President Ronald Reagan appointed her to the Supreme Court in 1981.

ROSIE O'DONNELL (b. 1962) The

daughter of an Irish immigrant father and an Irish American mother, Rosie O'Donnell is a successful talk show host, actor, and comedian.

Born in Commack, New York, O'Donnell broke into show business as a stand-up comic. Her Emmy Award–winning talk show, *The Rosie O'Donnell Show*, aired from 1996 to 2002. She has also performed on Broadway and in television and movies.

GEORGIA O'KEEFFE (1887–1986)

Wisconsin–born Georgia O'Keeffe was one of the United States's greatest painters. Her most famous works feature images of the

southwestern American landscape, especially animal bones, rocks, flowers, and desert scenes. O'Keeffe lived for many years in New York and later moved to New Mexico.

EUGENE O'NEILL (1888–1953)

Born in New York City, playwright Eugene O'Neill created many classic dramas, including *The Hairy Ape*, *A Moon for the Misbegotten*, and *The Iceman Cometh*. His most famous play is *Long Day's Journey into Night*. This work chronicles the struggles of an Irish American family, thought to be based on O'Neill's own family. O'Neill collected many honors for his work, including four Pulitzer Prizes and the Nobel Prize for Literature.

ED SULLIVAN (1902–1974)

A television pioneer, New York City–born Sullivan hosted his popular *Ed Sullivan Show* from 1948 to 1971. The weekly show, watched by millions of Americans every Sunday, helped launch the careers of many of the biggest acts in show business, including the Beatles and Elvis Presley.

JOHN L. SULLIVAN (1858–1918)

A hero to Irish Americans in the 1800s, John L. Sullivan was a bare-knuckle boxing champion in the days before boxers wore gloves. Sullivan held the heavyweight boxing title from 1882 to 1892. The child of Irish immigrants, he was born in Boston's heavily Irish Roxbury neighborhood.

LOUIS SULLIVAN (1856–1924)

Sullivan was a leading architect at the turn of the last century. He was born in Boston, the son of Irish immigrants, but later settled in Chicago. With his business partner, Dankmar Adler, Sullivan designed some of the nation's first skyscrapers. His most famous structures include Chicago's Carson Pirie Scott department store building and the Chicago Auditorium.

TIMELINE

ca. 6000 B.C.	Prehistoric settlers arrive in Ireland.
ca. 400	Celtic tribes conquer Ireland.
A.D. 432	Patrick, an English missionary, begins to convert the Irish to Christianity.
500s	According to legend, Saint Brendan sails from Ireland to North America.
800s	Vikings invade Ireland and establish towns along the coast.
1014	Brian Boru defeats the Vikings at Clontarf.
1160s	King Henry II of England invades Ireland.
1541	King Henry VIII of England declares himself king of Ireland.
1649	Oliver Cromwell puts down an Irish rebellion at Drogheda.
1700s	The English government enacts the Penal Laws, which strip Irish Catholics of their rights. Groups of Scotch-Irish from the northern part of Ireland settle in North America.
early 1800s	Small numbers of Irish Catholics begin to emigrate to North America.
1810	The *Shamrock*, the first Irish American newspaper, begins publication.
1836	The Ancient Order of Hibernians, based in Ireland, opens offices in the United States.

web enhanced at **www.inamericabooks.com**

1845–1850	Blight strikes the Irish potato crop; millions of people die of starvation or disease. Approximately 1.25 million Irish leave Ireland for America.
1852	Alarmed by Irish immigration, politicians form the American Party, nicknamed the Know-Nothing Party.
1855	New York establishes Castle Garden as an entry station for immigrants.
1861	The Civil War begins. Irish immigrants join military units on both sides, including the acclaimed Irish Brigade.
1863	Irish Americans riot against the draft in New York City.
1877	Nineteen Molly Maguires are hanged in western Pennsylvania.
1928	Irish Catholic Alfred Smith loses the presidential election to Herbert Hoover.
1949	The Republic of Ireland is established.
1960	John F. Kennedy is elected, becoming the first Catholic president of the United States.
late 1960s	The Troubles erupt in Northern Ireland.
1970s–1990s	Thousands of Irish move to the United States seeking employment.
1981	Milwaukee holds its first Irish Fest, which has grown to become the world's largest Irish festival.
2002	The Irish Hunger Memorial, honoring victims of the Great Famine, is dedicated in New York City.
2004	Bill Murray is nominated for an Academy Award for Best Actor for his role in *Lost in Translation*.

Glossary

BLIGHT: a disease that strikes plants, causing them to wither and die

EMIGRATE: to leave one's home country to live somewhere else. A person who emigrates is called an emigrant.

EVICTED: forced to leave one's home

GAELIC: the language of the ancient Irish Celts. Some modern Irish people speak Gaelic.

HIBERNIAN: relating to Ireland and the Irish

IMMIGRATE: to arrive to live in a new country. A person who immigrates is called an immigrant.

INTEGRATED: absorbed into mainstream society

POPE: the spiritual head of the Roman Catholic Church. Roman Catholics believe that the pope is Christ's chief representative on earth.

PROTESTANTISM: a major division of Christianity comprised of hundreds of different denominations. Unlike Roman Catholics, Protestants do not believe in the pope's authority.

QUARANTINE: to isolate people as a way to prevent the spread of disease

QUOTAS: limits on admission to a school, workplace, or other institution, usually based on religion, gender, race, or ethnicity

ROMAN CATHOLICISM: a major division of Christianity, governed by the pope in Rome

SCOTCH-IRISH: Scottish people who settled in Northern Ireland in the early 1600s. Many Scotch-Irish later emigrated to North America.

THINGS TO SEE AND DO

IRISH HERITAGE TRAIL, BOSTON, MASSACHUSETTS
<http://www.irishheritagetrail.com>
Boston has one of the largest Irish American communities in the nation, and the city holds many sites that are significant in Irish American history. Visitors to Boston can walk the Irish Heritage Trail and view such sites as the Rose Kennedy Rose Garden, an Irish famine memorial, and the JFK Library and Museum.

IRISH HUNGER MEMORIAL, NEW YORK, NEW YORK
<http://www.batteryparkcity.org/ihm.htm>
his open-air memorial to the victims of the Great Famine includes a quarter-acre replica of a mid-1800s Irish farm, complete with potato fields, stone walls, a fieldstone cottage, and plants and flowers native to County Mayo. The memorial also includes facts about the famine, along with lines from Irish poetry and song. Sculptor Brian Tolle designed the memorial, which is located in New York's Battery Park City.

JOHN FITZGERALD KENNEDY LIBRARY AND MUSEUM, BOSTON, MASSACHUSETTS
<http://www.cs.umb.edu/jfklibrary>
Dedicated to the memory of the nation's thirty-fifth president, this site features historic documents, photographs, audiovisual materials, and other items connected to John F. Kennedy's life and presidency. Museum exhibits shed light on the Kennedys—the "First Family" of Irish America.

MILWAUKEE IRISH FEST, MILWAUKEE, WISCONSIN
<http://www.irishfest.com>
The world's largest Irish festival takes place in the summer in Milwaukee, on the shores of Lake Michigan. More than 100,000 festivalgoers arrive each year to enjoy Irish music, step dancing, dramas, sporting contests, and more. Guests can attend music and dance workshops; eat Irish foods such as corned beef, cabbage, and soda bread; and purchase Irish collectibles and crafts. Organizations even help visitors trace their family trees back to Ireland.

OLD SAINT PATRICK'S CHURCH, CHICAGO, ILLINOIS
<http://www.oldstpats.org>
Founded by Irish immigrants on Easter morning 1846, Old Saint Patrick's is a Chicago landmark and a symbol of Chicago's Irish community. The building was constructed in the 1850s. Visitors to the church can admire the impressive architecture and decorations, including fifteen beautiful stained-glass windows. Installed between 1912 and 1922, the windows were inspired by Celtic art. In 1977 Old Saint Patrick's was listed on the National Register of Historic Places.

SAINT PATRICK'S DAY PARADE, NEW YORK, NEW YORK
The largest Saint Patrick's Day parade in the nation, New York's parade features more than 150,000 marchers each year. Irish American soldiers organized the first parade in 1766. Later, Irish benevolent societies joined together to host the event. Every year, military units, bands of Irish musicians, and groups such as the Ancient Order of Hibernians are prominent among the marchers.

SOURCE NOTES

7   "To Welcome Paddy Home" (traditional), Boys of the Lough, *Thousands Are Sailing: Irish Songs of Immigration*, Shanachie Entertainment Corporation, compact disc 78025.

11   "Shamrock Shore" (traditional), Karan Casey, *Thousands Are Sailing: Irish Songs of Immigration*,

Shanachie Entertainment Corporation, compact disk 78025.

15   Helen Selina (Countess of Dufferin), "Lament of the Irish Emigrant" in *The Oxford Anthology of English Poetry*, vol. 2, ed. John Wain (New York: Oxford University Press, 1986), 351–353.

22 G. Bernard Shaw, *Man and Superman: A Comedy and Philosophy* (Cambridge, UK: Cambridge University Press, 1903), 150.

24 Laxton, *Famine Ships,* 10.

25 Cecil Woodham-Smith, *The Great Hunger: Ireland, 1845–1849* (London: Penguin Books, 1991), 217.

31 Edward Laxton, *The Famine Ships: The Irish Exodus to America* (New York: Henry Holt and Company, 1996), 165–166.

39 "Pat Murphy of the Irish Brigade" (traditional), Mick Moloney, *Far from the Shamrock Shore,* Shanachie Entertainment Corporation, compact disk 78050.

50 Michael Coffey, ed., *The Irish in America,* (New York: Hyperion, 1997), 154.

51 Tom Collins Jr., telephone conversation with author, August 21, 2002.

56 Phyllis Gaffney Fifield, conversation with author, August 20, 2002.

SELECTED BIBLIOGRAPHY

BOOKS

Coffey, Michael, ed. *The Irish in America*. New York: Hyperion, 1997. This well-illustrated book looks at the Irish American community in detail, including its churches, political achievements, employment history, and role in the arts. Prominent Irish Americans contribute illuminating essays to the collection.

Cooper, Brian E. *The Irish American Almanac and Green Pages*. Rev. ed. New York: Harper and Row Publishers, 1973. A guidebook to Irish life in the United States, this book catalogs Irish toasts, proverbs, and superstitions; discusses Irish words and names; helps Irish Americans search for their roots; and introduces famous Irish Americans. It includes a directory of Irish American businesses and organizations.

Greeley, Andrew M. *The Irish Americans: The Rise to Money and Power*. New York: Harper and Row Publishers, 1981. Greeley examines the Irish American community, from its roots in Ireland to its status in the late 1900s. He focuses on the Irish character and how the community as a whole found success in the United States.

Laxton, Edward. *The Famine Ships: The Irish Exodus to America*. New York: Henry Holt and Company, 1996. For many Irish who fled the Great Famine for Canada and the United States, the voyage across the Atlantic was almost as bad as the misery they left behind in Ireland. Thousands died on the "famine ships"—both at sea and upon reaching North American ports. Laxton examines these ships and the fate of their passengers.

Woodham-Smith, Cecil. *The Great Hunger: Ireland, 1845–1849*. London: Penguin Books, 1991. A detailed account of the terrible famine, this book examines the political and economic aspects of the disaster, the specifics of the potato blight, the plight of the starving Irish, and the details of immigration to America.

The Irish in America: Long Journey Home. Four Parts. Walt Disney Studios in association with WGBH Boston, 1995. This four-part documentary examines the Irish American experience through interviews, archival film footage, music, and still photographs. Part I looks at the Great Famine and the initial wave of immigration. Part II details the early Irish community in the United States. Part III looks at the Kennedy family and its rise to success and power. Part IV explores the life and work of Eugene O'Neill, the great Irish American playwright.

FURTHER READING & WEBSITES

NONFICTION

Anderson, Catherine Corley. *John F. Kennedy.* Minneapolis: Lerner Publications Company, 2004. This biography profiles the life and times of President John F. Kennedy. Filled with black and white period photographs, the book details his early years, his service as U.S. senator and U.S. president, and the assassination that ended his life.

Bartoletti, Susan Campbell. *Black Potatoes: The Story of the Great Irish Famine, 1845–1850.* Boston: Houghton Mifflin Company, 2001. Drawing on first-person accounts, historical documents, and contemporary newspaper images, this book tells the story of the famine that devastated Ireland in the late 1840s—and sent more than one million Irish across the Atlantic to seek a new life in America.

Beller, Susan Provost. *Never Were Men So Brave: The Irish Brigade during the Civil War.* New York: Margaret K. McElderry Books, 1998. This book examines the famed Irish Brigade, the all-Irish unit that fought bravely for the Union during the Civil War. Beller describes the brigade's role in some of the war's most important battles, examines its leader, Thomas Meagher, and discusses the great famine that led so many Irish people to America a decade before the war.

Hoobler, Dorothy, and Thomas Hoobler. *The Irish American Family Album*. Introduction by Joseph P. Kennedy II. New York: Oxford University Press Children's Books, 1998. Citing oral history sources, letters, and memoirs, the authors present the Irish American experience—from the Great Famine in Ireland to resettlement in the United States. Photographs and engravings shed additional light on the lives of the immigrants.

James, Simon. *The World of the Celts*. New York: Thames & Hudson, 1993. This richly illustrated book examines the lives and culture of the Celts—the ancient inhabitants of Ireland and northern Europe. Although written for adults, the book will appeal to readers of all ages.

January, Brendan. *Ireland*. New York: Children's Press, 1999. This book provides an overview of Irish geography, history, and culture. Color photographs and extensive back matter offer additional insight into the Irish nation.

Josephson, Judith Pinkerton. *Mother Jones: Fierce Fighter for Workers' Rights*. Minneapolis: Lerner Publications Company, 1997. As a child in Ireland, Mary Harris "Mother" Jones witnessed oppression of the Irish firsthand. After immigrating to the United States, she devoted her life to fighting for the rights of workers, especially children. This book tells her story.

Severin, Tim. *The Brendan Voyage*. New York: Modern Library, 2000. Who was the first European to reach America? Many think it was Saint Brendan of Ireland, said to have crossed the Atlantic in the A.D. 500s. In this book (written for adults but accessible to all readers), Severin describes how he built a boat just like Brendan's and set out to re-create Brendan's voyage. His success in reaching North America proves that Brendan might have done so as well.

FICTION

Daly, Ita. *Irish Myths and Legends*. New York: Oxford University Press, 2001. Novelist Daly retells ten traditional Irish tales using a modern voice.

Magical illustrations by Bee Willey help bring the ancient stories to life.

Nolan, Janet. *The St. Patrick's Day Shillelagh.* Morton Grove, IL: Albert Whitman & Co., 2002. On Saint Patrick's Day, a modern American girl named Kayleigh finds a shillelagh, or club, that has been passed down from one of her ancestors, an Irish immigrant. Along with receiving the shillelagh, Kayleigh learns the story of her family's history.

Schneider, Mical. *Annie Quinn in America.* Minneapolis: Carolrhoda Books, Inc., 2001. Victims of the terrible potato famine, twelve-year-old Annie and her brother leave Ireland to join their sister in New York. This historical novel tells of Annie's struggles as she departs her homeland and begins a new life in the United States.

WEBSITES

ANCIENT ORDER OF HIBERNIANS IN AMERICA
<http://www.aoh.com>
The AOH is one of the largest and oldest Irish American organizations. Its website reports on the group's activities and offers links to many other Irish and Irish American sites and organizations.

INAMERICABOOKS.COM
<http://www.inamericabooks.com>
Visit www.inamericabooks.com, the on-line home of the In America series, to get linked to all sorts of useful information. You'll find historical and cultural websites related to individual groups as well as general information on genealogy, creating your own family tree, and the history of immigration in America.

THE IRISH ECHO ONLINE
<http://www.irishecho.com>
The *Irish Echo,* founded in 1928, is the leading Irish American newspaper in the country. Geared toward recent Irish immigrants, the paper covers the news from Ireland, as well as issues of interest to the Irish in the United States.

IRISH FAMILY HISTORY FOUNDATION
<http://www.irishroots.net>
Using church records, government documents, and other listings, the foundation helps people from all over the world trace their Irish roots.

INDEX

ACKNOWLEDGMENTS: THE PHOTOGRAPHS IN THIS BOOK ARE REPRODUCED WITH THE PERMISSION OF: © Digital Vision, pp. 1, 3, 18; © Courtesy of Historic Impressions, www.historicimpressions.com, p. 6; © North Wind Picture Archives, pp. 7, 12, 46, 63 bottom left; © Gianni Dagli Orti/CORBIS, p. 8; © The Art Archive/The Art Archive, p. 10; Library of Congress, pp. 11 (LC–USZ62–078308), 19 (LC–USZ62–103231), 23 (LC–USZ62–105528), 24 (LC–USZ62–103220), 30 (LC–USZ62–127764), 32, 34 (LC–USZ62–118126), 35 (LC–USZ62–19431), 37 (LC–USZC4–4605), 38 (LC–USZC4–1619), 40 (LC–USZ62–47036), 41, 49 (LC–USZ62–108119), 62 right (LC–USZ62–111780), 63 top right (LC–USZ62–126318), 63 bottom right (LC–USZ62–080122), 66 left (LC–USZ62–086846), 66 bottom right (LC–USZ62–116606), 67 top left (LC–USZ62–124527), 67 bottom left (LC–USZ62–123391), 67 top right (LC–USZ62–119896); © The Art Archive/British Library/British Library, p. 13; © by Courtesy of the National Park Service, Ellis Island Immigrant Museum, p. 15; © James Marrinan, p. 16; © CORBIS, p. 20; © Brown Brothers, pp. 26, 48; © From Friedrich Kapp: Immigration and the Commissioners of Emigration of the State of New York, 1870, p. 27; © Northern Pacific Railroad, p. 29; © Independent Picture Service, p. 42; © National Archives, p. 43 (102–LH–1941); © The Newberry Library, p. 44; © The Historical Society of Pennsylvania (HSP), Balch Institute for Ethnic Studies, p. 45; © Bettmann/CORBIS, pp. 50, 53 (bottom); © The John F. Kennedy Library, pp. 52 (PC8), 53 top (ST–C237–1–63); © Imperial War Museum, London, p. 54; © Express News/ Hulton|Archive, p. 55; © Milwaukee Irish Fest, p. 57; © Photofest, pp. 58, 63 top left, 65 top left; © Sandy Felsenthal/CORBIS, p. 60; © Dictionary of American Portraits, pp. 62 top left, 67 bottom right; © Hollywood Book & Poster, pp. 62 bottom left, 66 top right; © AP/Wide World Photos, p. 64 top left; © SportsChrome East/West, Rob Tringali, pp. 64 bottom left, 65 bottom left; © U.S. Senator John McCain, p. 64 right. Maps by Bill Hauser, pp. 9, 33.

Cover photos: The New York Public Library, Astor, Lenox and Tilden Foundations (top); Courtesy of Historic Impressions, www.historicimpressions.com (bottom); © Digital Vision (title, back cover).